"What Would the World be like without?"

Written By

Alfred Hasan Graham

This book is dedicated to my mother, Colleen Graham. Thank you for your knowledge and support. Without your love and sacrifice there would be no me.

For orders and Author Contact visit

4960Publishing.com

Follow us on Social Media @4960publishing

Share your experience on Instagram

Today seemed like a regular day for Wayne.

He woke up, brushed his teeth, and heard his mother call.

"Wayne, it's time for breakfast."

Wayne ran out the bathroom like a superhero.

He had quite the imagination.

"Mom, can I have some more syrup on my pancakes please?" asked Wayne.

"No, that's enough syrup. Now hurry up and finish your breakfast." Mom demanded.

"I'm finished." Wayne responded.

"No you're not, you haven't touched that oatmeal." Mom said.

"I don't want it." Wayne answered.

"Well, how else are you going to be big and strong?" Mom reminded him.

"Go get your book bag and meet me at the car." Wayne's mother ordered.

Mom grabbed the car keys and put the code into the security system just before locking the door.

On the ride to school, Wayne looked out of the window as he did everyday. When they got to a stoplight, suddenly, Wayne asked, "Ma! Who invented the stoplight?" "I'm not sure of his name honey, but I do know he was African American." Mom answered.

"Really " Wayne replied, surprised.

"Yes, don't be so surprised. When you get to school ask your teacher to give you a book on African American inventions." Mom suggested.

Wayne was shocked to hear that. He couldn't wait to get to school.

When Wayne's mother pulled up to the school, Wayne was in a rush to get out of the car but not before Mom said, "Give me a kiss!"

"Mom" Wayne whined as his mother gave him a big kiss. Wayne got out of the car and ran towards the school building. "Come straight home after school!" Mom yelled.

While Wayne was in school, he went to ask his favorite teacher, Mr. Green, about African American inventions.

"Excuse me Mr. Green." Wayne said tapping on Mr. Green from behind.

"Yes Wayne? How can I help you?" asked Mr. Green.

"I wanted to know… Do you have any books on African American inventions?" Wayne asked.

"I'm happy to hear you want to learn more about American history Wayne. One second… Here we go!" Mr. Green said as he handed Wayne an old book.

"Take this book but don't read it until you get home." Mr. Green ordered.

"Oh wow! Thanks Mr. Green!" Wayne excitedly replied.

Wayne was eager to read that book but, "I must follow Mr. Green's orders." He thought.

After school, Wayne spotted Dee running over to him asking "Hey Wayne! You want to go ride our bikes?"

Wayne replied, "Nah, I have something to do. I will see you later on."

"Alright" Dee replied with a puzzled look.

Wayne continued to walk home.

Once Wayne reached home, he rushed to his room and opened the book that Mr. Green had given him.

While reading it he paused to say, "Wow!! We invented a lot of things. The roller coaster, peanut butter, fire extinguisher, the list goes on and on." It wasn't long before Wayne wondered into the world of imagination just after saying to himself,

"What would the world be like without African American inventions?"

"Wake up! Wayne, wake up! It's time for school! Wash up and come down for breakfast." Mom demanded.

Wayne rose up out of bed rubbing his eyes.

Wayne walked into the bathroom.

"My hairbrush it's not here, that's weird." Wayne said.

Lynda Newman, an African American woman in the year 1898, invented the hairbrush.

Wayne started to rub his hair forward using his hand and finished getting ready for school. Once he was done, Wayne headed to the kitchen where another surprise awaited him.

Wayne ate his breakfast without much of a word and then suddenly he said,

"The refrigerator! It's not here!"

"Where is it?" He then asked.

"What are you talking about Wayne? You've been acting strange this morning." Wayne's mom answered. "But mom John Standard, an African American, invented the refrigerator on July 14th, 1891." cried Wayne. "That's Enough Wayne! Get your book bag and meet me at the car." Wayne's mother ordered as she grabbed the car keys.

"Excuse me, Mom." Wayne said.

"Yes Wayne?" She replied.

"Where is the security system?" He asked.

"What security system? I'm locking the door. That isn't enough?" She asked. "Oh no don't tell me…" Wayne whispered to himself while shaking his head. Wayne hadn't read far enough in the book to know that the home security system we have today was inspired by Marie Brown's 1969 home surveillance invention. Even so, he still had an idea as to why so many things were missing. By that moment, he knew he was living in a world without African American inventions. "This is going to be a long day." Wayne mumbled.

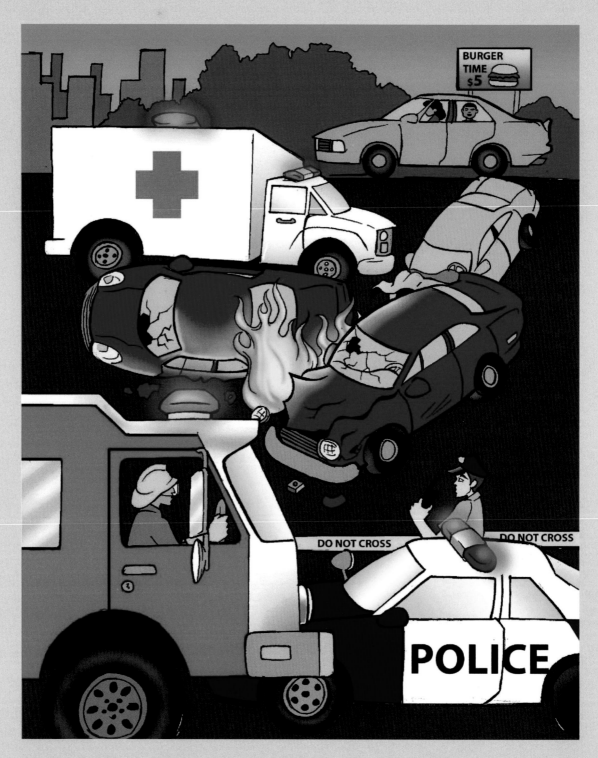

On the way to school there were no stoplights. Cars were backed up, horns were honking, and there were even a few crashes.

Garrett A Morgan invented the stoplight in the year 1922.

Wayne arrived at school and saw the janitor on his knees cutting the grass with a scissor like tool. He didn't have a lawn mower because John A. Burr invented it in 1899.

Once Wayne got inside the school building, he saw his reading teacher Ms. Parker walking up the steps.

Wayne remembered that usually Ms. Parker takes the elevator to class, but not today because Alexander Miles invented the elevator in 1877. Wayne started to feel how African American inventions made a lot of things easier for the world.

After school, on the walk home, Wayne was thinking about all the things that were missing until he saw his friend Dee.

"Hey Dee, what's up?" Wayne asked.

"Nothing much." Dee replied.

"Let's go ride our bikes." Wayne suggested.

"Bikes?" said Dee with a puzzled look. "Yeah, bikes. You asked me if I wanted to ride yesterday. Remember?" Wayne asked shockingly.

"Nah, don't remember. But we can go catch some grasshoppers." Dee responded.

"Catch, Grasshoppers!" Wayne shouted. "Oh! No!"

Wayne started to run home. He wanted to check the book and see if an African American invented the bicycle.

Wayne busted through the door to his house. "DOOP" went the door.

Once Wayne got back to his room, he scanned the book as he turned the pages.

"Here it is! The bicycle frame! Isaac R. Johnson invented it in 1899. I can't go on like this. Where are all the African American inventions? Where are they?"

Wayne started to twist and turn in his bed shouting, "No! No! No! No! This can't be! It just can't be!" He stopped dreaming from his mother shaking him saying, "Wayne, wake up, wake up. You must have been having a bad dream. Come on, it's time for school. You were reading that book until you fell asleep."

Wayne jumped out of bed, ran to the bathroom to check for his hairbrush.

"It's here!" He roared with excitement.

At the breakfast table Wayne told his mother about the dream he'd had. She replied, "That must have been an interesting experience Wayne."

"You're telling me." He replied. "I am so thankful for my ancestors and the things they invented for the world." Wayne explained.

"Well Wayne you should be. Always remember, you have the same ability." Mom Reminded.

More African American inventions

Invention	Inventor	Date	Patent #
Air Condition	Jones, F.M.	Dec. 7, 1954	2,696,086
Bathroom Tissue Holder	Kenner, M.B.	Oct. 19, 1982	4,354,643
Bicycle Frame	Johnson, I.R.	Oct. 10, 1899	634,823
Bottle	Richardson	Dec. 12, 1899	638,811
Carriage (for a child)	Richardson, W.H	June 18, 1889	405,599
Chair, Folding	Purdy/Sadgwar	June 11, 1889	405,117
Coin Changer	Bauer, J.A.	Jan. 20, 1970	3, 490, 571
Curtain Rod	Scottron, S.R.	Aug. 30, 1892	481, 720
Door Stop	Dorsey, O.	Dec. 10, 1878	210,764
Electric Railway	Woods, G.T.	July 29, 1901	667,110
Elevator	Miles, A	Oct. 11, 1887	371, 207
Envelope Seal	Leslie, F.W.	Sept. 21, 1897	590,325
Fire Extinguisher	Martin, T.J.	Mar. 26, 1872	125,063
Fountain Pen	Purvis, W.B.	Jan. 7, 1890	419,065
Gas Mask (safety hood)	Morgan, G.A.	Oct. 13, 1914	1,113,675
Gear Shift, Automatic	Spikes, R.B.	Dec. 6, 1932	1,889.814
Golf Tee	Grant, G.F.	Dec. 12, 1899	638,920
Guitar	Flemming, R.F.	March 3, 1886	338,727
Hair Brush	Newman, L.D.	Nov. 15, 1898	614,335
Horse Shoe	Brown, O.E.	Aug. 23, 1892	481,271
Ironing Board	Boone, S	April 26, 1892	473,653
Lawn Mower	Burr, J.A.	May 9, 1899	624,749
Lawn Sprinkler	Smith, J.W.	May 4, 1897	581,785
Lemon Squeezer	White, J.T.	Dec. 8, 1896	572,849
Lock	Martin, W.A.	July 23, 1889	407,738
Lubricator	McCoy, E.J.	May 27, 1873	139,407
Lubricator (steam engines)	McCoy, E.J.	July 2, 1872	129,843
Lunch Box (dinner pail)	Robinson, J	Feb. 1, 1887	356,852
Mail Box (letter box)	Downing, P.B.	Oct. 27, 1891	462,096
Mail Box, Street Box	Downing, P.B.	Oct. 27, 1891	462,096
Mop	Stewart, T.W.	June 13, 1893	499,402
Pencil Sharpener	Love, J.L	Nov. 23, 1897	594,114
Pressing Comb	Sammons, W	Dec. 21, 1920	1,362,823
Razor Strop	Grenon, H	Feb. 18, 1896	554,867
Refrigerator	Standard, J	July 14, 1891	455,891
Remote Control (T.V.)	Jackson, J.N.	Oct. 14, 1980	4,228,543
Roller Coaster	Woods, G.T.	Dec. 19, 1899	639,692
Security System	Brown, M.V.	Dec. 2, 1969	3,482,037
Shoe (upgrade)	Deitz, W.A.	April 30, 1867	612,008
Suspenders	Ross, A.L.	Nov. 28, 1899	638,068
Traffic Signal	Gorgan, G.A.	Feb. 22, 1922	1,936,996
Wrench	Johnson, J.A.	Apr. 18, 1922	1,413,121

reference; uspto.gov